POEMS OF Z

POEMS OF Z

Paul Hyland

*Janet
from Paul & Z.*

BLOODAXE BOOKS

Copyright © Paul Hyland 1982
All rights reserved

ISBN: 0 906427 44 4

First published 1982 by
Bloodaxe Books Ltd,
P.O. Box 1SN
Newcastle upon Tyne NE99 1SN.

The publisher acknowledges the financial assistance
of Northern Arts.

Acknowledgements are due to the editors of *New Poetry 5*
(Hutchinson/Arts Council—P.E.N., 1979) and *South West
Review*, where some of these poems first appeared, and to
BBC Radio 3, and Shaun MacLoughlin who produced a
selection for broadcasting.

Typesetting & cover printing by
Tyneside Free Press Workshop Ltd, Newcastle upon Tyne.

Printed in Great Britain by
Unwin Brothers Ltd, Old Woking, Surrey.

VI

The pigs stay at home
I wade the English shores
where bum and back empty
with the great sawers called men

Or I dive in the deep waters
— one of my elements —
tearing oysters from their beds
like drowned corroded fruit

They are hard nuts to crack
with calloused brown hands
and a stainless knife's
sharp point, broad haft
I have prised a chuck
hundreds
The years, a stinking midden
The pearls, mostly small & grey
I send home to the pigs

Ears dulled that wonder
The shells a heap of deaf ears —
Now I sift through their clatter
clutching them at my head,
listening for the voice of my father

VII

Beneath that heap of shells
my father points downhill
to tell me that it runs
through another country
all the way to the sea

The sea trips off his tongue
like gossip — he has not seen it
but he knows it's worth talking about
— it is salty, he says
and larger than all the land

I lie dreaming of it
its smell comes up through knots
in the floorboards
from bacon curing under rafters
under my bed

With cows on the mountain
I sniff for it but have
to face the mountain
when it comes from
when rain from the sea falls

Nothing, not thunder, not flood
not cataract prepared me
for the raw deep voice of it
under the deck, the bellowing
of her who bore me on her
breast

Pages from Z's notebook

PREFACE

It will be clear why it is difficult for me to disclose how these poems came into my possession. Their unexpectedness and their unexpected power, that made such an impact on me, are the important things about them. In any case, I have nothing illuminating to say about their background, for all my knowledge of it comes from them. All I have is a small, rather dog-eared notebook of forty unlined pages, each with a poem pencilled upon it in English. The dedication and the quotations from Lear and Jonson are scribbled inside the front cover. At the head of the first page is written *Poems of Z*.

In passing Z's notebook to the publisher I have become involved in preparing the poems for the press. When he made revisions Z's usual practice was, it seems, to erase the original—'pencil stitched/and smudged across a grubby page'—but where he has not done this I have taken the two readings as alternatives, and have chosen the one I judged the better. I have also made a small handful of amendments to Z's sparse punctuation, for the sake of clarity or consistency.

Z seems to have been engaged in intelligence activities in the U.K. for a number of years. The poems are certainly about that, but I think it unlikely that our counter-espionage service will glean much from these pages. The poet—for this is what, in a crisis of self-examination, Z became—is not concerned with 'Names and Places/Technical Detail, Plans/Political Praxis, Miscellaneous'; he asks 'What does the heart know', and writes of his own tenderness and violence, duplicity and openness, his faithlessness and spiritual hunger. From his world within our world, employing our language, he casts a cool eye on England, 'the England I love'. He speaks movingly of the world of his childhood; the spy remembers his father and writes:

> . . . all the seasons
> gone for which he, his weathered face
> upturned, gathered intelligence

Here we have an extraordinary view of an extraordinary poetic development. The start must have been tentative, but once assured of what he was about I feel sure that Z wrote the poems as they stand in the notebook, one after another, each dependent on the one before, each qualified by the next. They demonstrate a sharpening of vision and a hardening of intention probably unsuspected at the outset. The naivety of the enterprise was to Z, I think, an essential element of it. Its success was perhaps as much of a surprise to him as it is to us. He felt it was not attainable in his own language. That Z should write so well in English is surely remarkable, but it is also crucial to his purpose:

> I need decode the words
> I do it in English
> I adopt that tongue

Towards the end he anticipates returning home and recalls M*** (an informant?) who returned 'from the fascists' hands' with his tongue cut out:

> muscles at his tongue's
> root fought with the air
> in his open mouth
>
> a crock at the end
> of an arc of blood.
> We cried out for him

Z has left us forty poems.

PAUL HYLAND

POEMS OF Z

*– in memory of my father who knew how to talk
and of my mother who knew how to sing*

*'Thou whoreson zed! thou
unnecessary letter!'*
　　　　　　– Lear

*'Z is a letter often heard
amongst us, but seldome seene.'*
　　　　　　– Jonson

I

This is sudden
this to be a poet

A need my comrades
would scoff at
if they knew, scoff
in our own tongue –

You an agent
from a thriller's cover
you a blank face
under a black hat

You a poet—I say it
too in my own tongue

I need decode the words
I do it in English
I adopt that tongue
it moves differently
in my mouth, it swells

If across these pages
it speaks I will hand them
to my friend the professor
at S***, he will translate
back into my own tongue

That will not be sudden
that handing over
this notebook when it is full

II

This is like taking off clothes
heavy coats one at a time
each one less burden
the weight of keeping warm
gone in a room with oil-light
and water breathing in iron

That's what it's like shedding
clothes, hardware, braces,
trousers and at the end
no shame. No shame

In a room with oil-light
lying in elbow-warm water
the grown flesh fallen away
bathing in the iron bath
supported by my mother's arm
her free hand rinsing my limbs

She sings to me in my own tongue
songs I will forget in London
I pitch my gurgles back to her
my poems she can't understand

III

You see there is nothing
naive and sentimental as
a grown man with soft hands
and a calloused heart
starting out as poet

The idea of it anyway.
From my rented table
through the spacious grid
of sash windows I keep
watch on Georgian London

As I once spied from a pane
set into thick thatch
on my father in the yard
the pigs rooting, my sisters
walking out in the wood

when I should have been sleeping.
Opposite, the porticoes in line
the columns and pediments
all at once I am astonished
at the weight of masonry

I walk in and out of every day

IV

In the streets of language
I need no maps any more.
If I were to try words of love
my tongue would taste
of their dust and litter

Intimacy that is paid for –
after sleepless nights sometimes
street signs are foreign flags
pinned to great architecture
roads veer off at wrong angles

I am a beast turned drab
driven in from the far country
to scavenge in dustbins
and basement entries
tainted by offal and old bones

My lack of condition
my dullness is protective
colouration for mission
the noblest drive of my kind
to survive, depraved appetite

This pencil and paper
my belling bark that should
fly meadows and pierce woods
pitched off monstrous buildings
in the streets of language

V

As a boy I was one
learning to be more

One with the pigs in their pen
far inland chucking them acorns
from a holed bucket,
the sea a dream of passion

One with my sisters' boys
little man among little men
One with my aunt in town
in my white stiff things

One for my first communion
One for the party, party-man
In London now I am Legion
for we are many

I would invite my pigs here
for my first communion –
they would rush outwards
in all directions

And every English shore
they dashed themselves over
trotters gashing own throats
would wash with their gore

I would be one
I have learned to be more

VI

The pigs stay at home
I wade the English shores
where burns and becks empty
with great sewers called rivers

Or I dive in the deep waters
—one of my elements—
rouse oysters from their beds
like drowned corroded fruit

They are hard nuts to crack
with crabbed brown hands
and a stainless knife's
sharp point, broad haft

I unhinge and chuck hundreds
the years, a stinking midden
the pearls, mostly small and grey
I send home to the pigs

VII

Beneath that heap of shells
my father points downriver
to tell me that it runs
through another country
all the way to the sea

The sea trips off his tongue
like gossip—he has not seen it
but knows it's worth talking about
—it is salty he says
and larger than all the land

I lie dreaming of it
its smell comes up through
cracks in the floorboards
from bacon curing under
rafters under my bed

With cows on the riverbank
I sniff for it but turn
to face the mountains
where it comes from
where rain from the sea falls

Nothing, not thunder, not flood
nor cataract prepared me
for the raw deep voice of it
under the deck, the lullaby
of her who bore me on her breast

Years dulled that wonder
the shells a heap of deaf ears.
Now I sift through their clatter
clutching them at my head
listening for the voice of my father

VIII

I creep nearer and nearer
—my sisters hide their faces
even safe inside the house –
the nuzzled ground slavers
and sucks at my shoes

I creep close to my father
and his friend G***
and the pale pig standing
bound between them
father shaving its throat

A quick sliced stab and blood
—though I know it trickled
I see it spurt in an arc
a thick monotonous rainbow
caught in a crock

The arc of the pig's scream
stopped in my ears—
ten minutes before silence
trotters trying to flail
blond eyelashes still

Only when the blood stops
at last I start to cry
a complicated wailing
father reproves with his glare
to my sisters' scorn I creep away

IX

That was the first time
I approached slow death
under a waxing moon

Father's apprentice, I know
the pig's swan-song well
never two the same

I know it well, I feel it
coming from the throat
the beast's strain in my hands

My hands shake as I write
I can't translate, in English
I cannot make you hear it

X

My mother's stitchery
by oil-light, bright needle
pricking linen with petals
taut as a tambourine
beneath tight black eyes

Come quick, my father calls
come do something useful.
She anchors the skein
who never did anything
not useful, but this

They kneel down together
in the sty by oil-light
the feverish sow between them
a small sister, brown hands
travelling her white lard

Your mother was beautiful
father tells me one day.
It is a strange saying.
His eyes that have known more
than mine seem to see less

That fine work by oil-light
he tells her, wrinkles your eyes
but occasions for it
don't stop, nor she, save to suck
new silk for the needle's eye

All her care is dispersed
now, given or gone away
under some several roofs
my sisters and I
all her useless stitchery

XI

I have a piece here in London
made of stitches I cannot name
in English, let alone my tongue

A blue bird perched on a green branch
among red blooms but faded, old
linen yellowed at every fold

It is like my heart, packed, unpacked
furled and unfurled in foreign rooms
hid in the luggage of my limbs

On my table in this blank book
I trace the profile of that heart
with pencil, rubber and no art

In this ageing and English light
it's hard to read, too dark at times
to write, seeing so little rhymes

Or too much chimes unjustly –
were they all silken lies she told
that are now mellowed and grown old

This one, hung in my tall white room
stretched again, gilt-framed and fading
dimmed by the light I see it in

The light I work by, pencil stitched
and smudged across a grubby page
dazzles my eyes with the heart's rage

XII

And each plough-time the heavy horse
leans at unbroken ground, the share
burnished of rust at the first turn
first furrow, the year's paradigm

The soil's breath breaks intact from it
and birds hang on its lips, I pass
en route for school and my return
sees father's warp stretched hedge to hedge

I learn my letters, figures too
he broadcasts over harrowed land
I weave between the feint ruled lines
his testament, my exercise

At home my head buried in books
The first cuckoo! my father calls
Can you hear it? Of course I can
I do not know why I say no

I am bored with the grand routine
that feeds me, the man who works it.
My hunger is for print; his, corn
in stitch, weather's embroidery

His labour is all harvested
sewing unpicked, all the seasons
gone for which he, his weathered face
upturned, gathered intelligence

XIII

There is one place I know
where the street smells right
in Soho, a café where I go
sometimes, where they sell
the right sort of bread

and where they speak my tongue
among themselves. I listen
with the other foreigners
the English men, I sink
my teeth in the bread

and roll it on my tongue
how sourdough sweetens!
and swallow it hard

XIV

The priest throws back his head
under the uptilted chalice

Under the black of his beard
his supple throat pumps

As if he emptied the dome
of the psalms lapping its brim

And on my tongue dissolution
of wafer and high seriousness

The creed's sumptuous chant
strangely bland but indigestible

Because I think I could not give
all my juices to it; flatus

In the bowel lent a pained smile
to the practice of holiness

To him whose racked form rode the tree
into whose death I could not donate

Suffering so framed with pomp
but I see now in retrospect

Not wholly corrupt, a memory
a drinking to certain hope

The priest's voluptuous throat
throbbing with joyous guffaws

Celebrating a death and again
roaring at the death of death

XV

Then I was consecrated
to correct economics
I was a bright pupil

Now with a dull eye
I look out from London
across foothills of brick

Domes and spires diminished
douched by a cataract
of glass, architect's vision

I had it, I saw man
pinned on the drawing board
in plan and elevation

My tall head built of panes
tears of glass sizzled
on the dome of my heart

Theoretical pity
for the man I had seen
not for me, not for me

I had not yet learned that.
I was a bright pupil.
Now with a dull eye

I creep through porticoes
pitiful, not a cubit
added to my stature

XVI

(Is it worth it
this dredging up
memories of

the future that
is long gone and
that never was?

Worth anything
to think of the
position to

which ambition
raised me, me and
all of mankind

it imagined?
Since I have been
put in my place

probably it
is worthless but
it is costly)

XVII

I was a saint, for love
of country I left it –
frontiers as are well known
are imaginary
and bloody—my ideals
in the safe custody
of trustworthy comrades

Like a child who's lent
toys to fickle friends
I fear to return

What of my toys amongst
the pieces they picked up
the imaginary
and ransacked nursery
pieced together again
piecemeal, beloved country
ramshackle in my head

I want to visit
but I hesitate
to go back, for good

XVIII

The ship I came on
passport to mission
iron link with home
(the farewell handprint
of my dead father
on its starboard rail)
the subtle groundswell
sickness at parting
embarking upon
something

        When I heard
(from fellow-exiles
I can't call comrades)
that the vessel C***
survivor of war
by accident, had
long been broken up
steep deck, raucous plates
all scrap, in a gust
old salt stung my eyes

XIX

My sentimentality appals me
then consoles; emotions still, but sudden
I butter-fingered drop them and mis-feel

I was a hard nut in my prime to crack
a mind and body bedded snugly in
well knitted joints, nothing rotten or loose

But then a place grew softly where they met
back of the throat, perhaps, above the heart
grew large and liquid, a soft centre, sac

Whose juice digests my thick skin from within
and now I think my insides are all slops
contained tears pent up in a fragile shell

I am a hard man before breaking out
I shall, if I hole myself, leak away.
I am appalled, to hatch now is to die

XX

I do not listen much
to fellow-exiles' tales
of home, they must believe
they are better off here
since they cannot return

I do not listen much
because I can, but one
such bitter recital
nestles deep in my ear
like a worm, a tale of

imaginative torture –
a troublesome priest penned
in B*** prison, at length
exhorted by a spike
red hot steel up his arse

on his knees to say mass
over shit and piss
though ordure and urine
were the words the man used
who told the tale, shaking

I don't know if I should
take his words for gospel
his imagination
or my lack of it, fact
it is best to forget

Facts are made up. To know
from far, to remember
is to daydream. Bread. Shit.
To see straight in close-up
an imaginative act

XXI

I have nothing to say in return
missionary without a gospel

lamp hid under a bushel
me in this airless room!

you think I've escaped to this
from the pig-pen, my trampled country

or am expatriate on greener grass
mixing my hopes and fears with yours

my conversation is a charade
I watch from under word-cover

when I re-enter my homeland
I shall shout hopes out loud

I'm no exile banished from my soil
exile is my mission

patriot, servant, soon I shall return
till then this pencil is blunted

re-sharpened, otherwise never share
my fears with anyone, anywhere

XXII

My parents' business
always was well-known
in the next village
before ours because
our clear-eyed neighbour
silent Mother K***

had a garrulous
sister living there
to whom each Sunday
she'd carefully walk
with white eggs and take
brandy in return

retracing her steps
with a happily
empty basket just
as her darling hens
were cackling over
their darling white eggs

XXIII

Prayer was often difficult
the confessional was an easy route
to God's ear—it was his eye
I feared glinting through lattice-work

The presumptive photo of me
was taken before my first communion
crisp and black and white—his eye
an open shutter between prayers

snapping at each new secret sin
a series of mug-shots falling away
from the primal image—I
tried to surprise myself in mirrors

to find out if anything showed
the complexion of my soul seeping through
an aperture—that his eye
would scan, find wanting and write down

I could not find words for my sins
I repented of faith in forgiveness
penance mere punishment—I
feared passing of notes and whispering

XXIV

The hospital
—me a boy
in a men's ward—
I love the whole
the real world

Stethoscopes read
universal tremors
world of diagnoses
screens dragged around
trivial atrocities

and unlikely cures
starched sheets and
disinfectant
covering up
for corruption

I love it all
the noise of life
silence of death
orchestrated
out of control

Doctors bending over
listening with
their instruments
their smiles and
their knowledge

or what is not worse
ignorance
I love it all
a museum
of living sicknesses

as I love England

XXV

In the England I love
I am visitor
I am listener
and collector

I step out stooping
from the sick-room
the confessional
and the hen-coop

With my stethoscope
my white coat
and a notebook
full of symptoms

With my micro-camera
under my cassock
with white eggs
cradled in my smock

XXVI

When the air though cold
hung heavily in the trees
I heard a pig's scream
and looked out—an arena
at the forest's edge
where a desperate dog-wolf
chased one of our young

A piglet runs like a cat
ears flat, stops so fast
with all its trotters dug in
grinning in its fear
that the grey beast overruns
and snarling turns back
on the pale scampering thing

Then it seems success
turns the pig's head from terror
to playfulness till
its squealing is with laughter
and the dog-wolf too
relaxes despite hunger
fangs sure then of lard

Whether or not I dreamt this
or saw in the flesh
circus at the forest's edge
when the air though cold
hung heavily in the trees
I heard the pig's scream
bubble softly and turn red

XXVII

What I am does not add up
then I think
that always there's a big bomb
in the air

Plane circling above England
on alert
ready to head east before
you can blink

All is in order up there
precision
double-checked triple-fail-safe
on target

Above smiling diplomats
governments
and people making mistakes
making love

I think of just one of them
just one crew
made one through harsh discipline
conditioned

Made interrogation-proof
by torture
dependable tools put through
my paces

I am of their brotherhood
I encode
the world's everyday chaos
my cover

When I wonder what I am
I think of
this life of ours, men plus bombs
I add up

XXVIII

I am not Samson
pillars and porticoes
do not give way
at my weight
I am not blind

I watch the faces
listen to gossip
corridors and closets
whispers of free speech
this democracy

A house divided
against itself
—eyes already
clogged with coin—
does not need Samson

XXIX

In my country
we look into each other's eyes
freedom has been won

The victors have given it to us
—if freedom is everything
that is what we owe them

When a man dies his son
eats the bacon that cures
under the dead man's rafters

The chandelier's contagion inherited
by blood: the victors' heirs
preserve our freedom, salt it down

We are hungry
the flesh of our house whole
but divided in spirit

We look into each other's eyes
first one way and then another
first one way and then another

XXX

I am a puppet
on very long strings

length gives a certain
elasticity

Or

I am a part of
a ventriloquist's act

I sit very still
and keep my mouth shut

I am a dummy
on the knee of a

cadaver

XXXI

My face a professional dissident
I stretch to fit the mask

My heart a muscle-knot
can't afford feeling
acts by the method
—empathy disallowed—
objective performance
happy when the audience
turns away, coughs behind its hand

My head a cabinet
of files each labelled
Faces, Names and Places
Technical Detail, Plans
Political Praxis, Miscellaneous
classified according to
priority and secrecy

Watch, listen to the audience
collate
designate
transmit
adrenalin
instinct
the head gathers intelligence

The face knows nothing
the heart knows something else

XXXII

What does the heart know
it is not certain

the heart is in exile
and not from its soil

Voltaire's tragic figure
the faithless priest

the heart thought it escaped
God and his trappings

left home for the night
like my grown sisters

drowning the pigs' musk
with toilet water

carrying their smart shoes
as far as the road

lodging boots in the hedge
against their return

the heart has grown up twice
faithless atheist

Materialism & History
are not enough

I want more I want more
the hungry heart

I know about hunger
when there is no food

but no, not when there is
no such thing as food

XXXIII

Lately, perhaps because I soon shall cross it
for the last time, I have been tripping
to the sea

And what seems like a mote troubles my eye
a man's head floating far out, fighting
with the sea

Imaginary and bloody frontier –
stones, fine red fronds like hands' veins
in the sea

Unaccounted-for corpuscles per cubic metre
and only great mammals warming the dilute blood
of the sea

I pick up soft pebbles of chalk, sculpture
burrowed-in, bored-through, dense with the dead
of the sea

My size is embarrassing suddenly, my pride –
what do I know of the creaturely galaxies
in the sea

And what of the man I imagine
far out, trampled in the waves' charge, drowning
in the sea

I know nothing, I turn back to the low cliffs
their dirty-red and grey houses blindly looking
out to sea

And I think I throw my shoes off and dive in
a good socialist or a bourgeois hero
by the sea

My victim does not appreciate the difference
I buoy him up, he cries Save me, save me
from the sea

XXXIV

Soon I shall board a plane
and fly from one language
to another. It will
take a part of a day

I shall fly from English
even from these poems
back to my tongue. I still
think of it in that way

All my intelligence
flew that route under wraps
and waits for me. There I'll
be day by day by day

Transmitted, translated
back in time to the tongue
I was taught in. The thrill
of seeing, then, one way

Before that, older games
of dreams and sense and faith
long forgotten. My skill
with each word a new toy

I'll think of my poems
this intelligence in
my other tongue. I will
not be a sad old boy

XXXV

I am flying to my homeland
I will not be a sad old boy

My father is long dead
I will not be a sad old boy

My mother is dead also
I will not be a sad old boy

My sisters are still alive
I will not be a sad old boy

My wife is not any more
I will not be a sad old boy

My work is over and done with
I will not be a sad old boy

My time is up it is too late
I will not be a sad old boy

My time is my own
I will not be a sad old boy

What time?
I will not be a sad old boy

I've been saying it over and over
like a charm, a strong charm
repeated under a waxing moon
or litany, endless litany
chanted to ward off the devil
or a prayer, a heart-felt prayer
a begging letter

XXXVI

(Fortunately from
an objective viewpoint
I am unimportant

I serve the state
a people's monk
an eye on a stalk

my feelings and my fate
the last things
I should think about

I look out for the rest
why worry them
with my hope and guilt

I am unimportant
it takes so many me's
to make a mass)

XXXVII

I have not mentioned it yet
—a man in my position
has to be discreet with women—
but since I left my wife behind
a succession of at best
brief happinesses has dogged me

I think of my mother and father.
My eyes have known more than theirs
but seem to see less. I do not
wonder at my heaviness.
Eyes' saturated humours
precipitate a callus on the nerve

that only tears can solve.
However tenderly it was done
it has all been snatched and stashed
in the memory. Nothing was made.
Now I want to make it up
with somebody, in my tongue, at home

XXXVIII

What shall I say now
with this English tongue
cut out of my head

(M*** whom we thought lost
came back from the dead
from the fascists' hands

He had lost his tongue.
They had translated
him into a fool

forgetting how well
fools are listened to,
his eloquent hands

muscles at his tongue's
root fought with the air
in his open mouth

a crock at the end
of an arc of blood.
We cried out for him)

I have not suffered
not really, I am
it seems in one piece

and if we're careful
my friend, professor
at S***, will translate

all this, this false start
back into my tongue.
I may find my tongue

XXXIX

During the war—
men at men's throats
—how we trusted
our poor neighbours
we thought we knew
who our friends were

So I'll propose
a special vote
of thanks to friends
here in England
for trusting me—
here's to neighbours!

Do not disturb
was my watchword—
if he'll forgive
a spy's foibles
I'll forgive the
drunkard next door

Leave him in peace

XL

On leaving shall I pronounce
as retiring episkopos
benediction on my diocese?

Shall I quote Jesus, My peace
I leave with you? I would not bequeath
my whatever it is to a dog

In peace is passive enough,
your choice. Peace does not belong to me
I am going home to look for it

Shall I quote the prodigal,
Father I have sinned? I cannot tell
if I'm moving to or from the pig-pen

Because I'm taking myself with me
I'm taking myself to the banquet
I shall say grace

Paul Hyland was born in 1947 in Dorset. He read Biology and Philosophy at Bristol University and now works as a freelance writer in North Devon. His broadcast work includes the poem-sequence *Domingus* (with a sound-score by Barry Anderson), the drama-documentary *The Greatest Englishman*, and the play *Dancing Ledge* which was also toured by the Orchard Theatre as part of the Radio/Theatre '81 Festival.

His publications are *Riddles for Jack* (Northern House Poets, 1978), *Domingus* (Mid-Day Publications, 1978) and *Purbeck: The Ingrained Island* (Gollancz, 1978 & 1981).